Cooking with Steve

AND RONNIE

Book Cover by Julian Nicholson

Illustrations by Virág György

Recipes by Lynn Edwards

Book Design by Julian Nicholson and Rachael Wheeler

Stories by Julian Nicholson

1st edition 2023

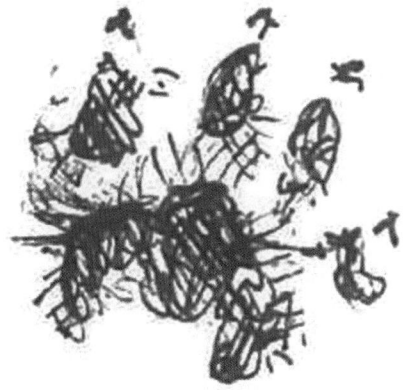

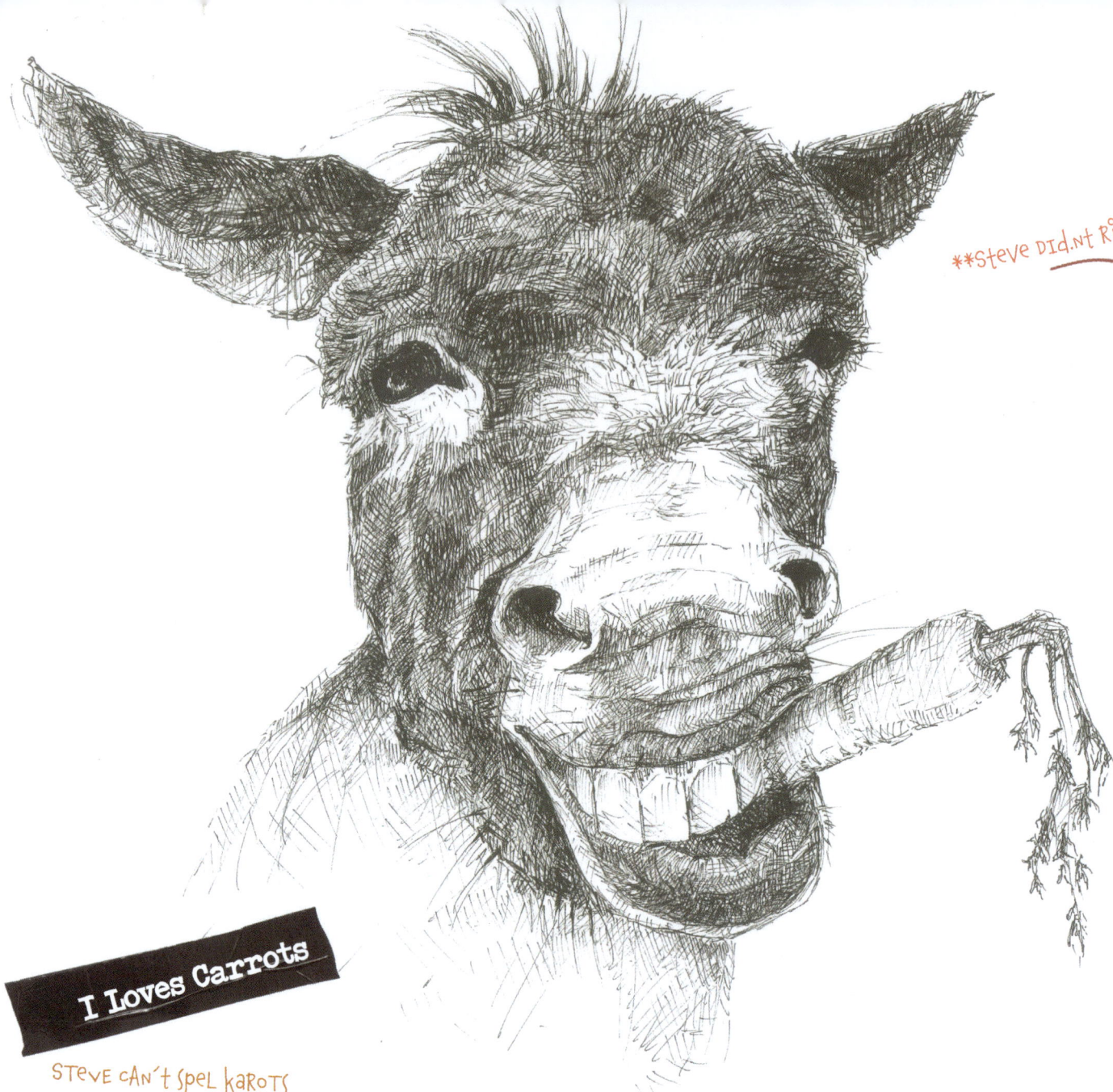

steve did.nt rite this

I Loves Carrots

steve can't spel karots

SPRING ONION
CARROT FRITTERS
AND

THESE ARE SO EASY AND YOU CAN MIX AND MATCH TO CREATE YOUR OWN PERSONAL FRITTER!

This has got Carrots in it

Put the onions, carrots, flour and seasoning into a bowl. Add the baking powder and now mix with the plant based milk to get a thick consistency.

Add a cup at a time until you get the right consistency. Use more or less as needed but it should be of a thick consistency and a mix that will hold its shape. Now mix in your lemon juice (this activates the baking powder and helps your fritters to "fluff" up)

Carefully heat up your oil and when it is at temperature (drop in a little of the mixture it should sizzle immediately) place in, carefully, spoonfuls of the mix, around the size of an ice cream scoop or a tablespoon.

Allow them to cook gently, turning them halfway through, when they are golden, and then place onto kitchen roll to drain and into a warm oven whilst you cook the rest.

Serve with a salad, noodles or with rice and a sauce of your choice. You can change the carrot and onion to your own taste, try courgettes and lemon for something a little different but a brilliant way to use up those leftover vegetables in your fridge.

I'm beterer THAN Steve

NOTES

1 Bunch of finely chopped spring onions (scallions) include the green part!
5 Grated carrots
200 gms / 1 cup Gram Flour
(You can use any flour but this will make them gluten free)
2 teaspoons of baking powder.
1 ½ Cups of plant based milk
Juice of 1 lemon
Teaspoon of paprika
1 chopped clove of garlic or a teaspoon of ready chopped.
Salt and Pepper
Vegetable oil to cook.

You can make and freeze these, just pop into a hot oven to heat through before eating. They also work really well sliced and put into a fresh, crunchy bread roll with salad and mayo!

MAKE YOUR OWN TOFU

THIS IS VERY EASY AND ONCE YOU GET STARTED ON THIS YOU CAN BEGIN TO CREATE YOUR OWN PERSONAL TOFU!

INGREDIENTS

1 Litre of soya milk (only use soya milk)
1 Tablespoon of apple cider vinegar
1 Large piece of muslin cloth

METHOD

Pour your soya milk into a saucepan and heat until simmering. Now stir in your apple cider vinegar.

It will separate and this is what you are looking for (same principle as curds and whey) Remove from the heat and then pour through your muslin cloth to keep the solids but dispose of the liquid.

Bring the cloth together and squeeze hard to get rid of as much liquid as you can. Now, at this stage you can shape your tofu into a mould (we use a bread tin) and leave to set in your fridge.

You now have home made tofu!
Notes
You can add flavouring at the heating of the milk stage so you can add herbs, garlic, paprika, black pepper in fact anything you want. You can also roll the tofu in dried herbs before you put into a mould, just create your own special tofu!

SCRAMBLED "EGG" TOFU

THE SECRET INGREDIENT TO THIS IS BLACK SALT. YOU CAN BUY THIS IN MOST ASIAN STORES OR ONLINE VERY EASILY BUT BE WARNED, YOU ONLY NEED A VERY SMALL AMOUNT SO GO EASY WITH IT!

INGREDIENTS

1 Block of firm tofu (must be firm)
1 teaspoon of black salt
1teaspoon of garlic powder
1 Tablespoon of nutritional yeast
1 teaspoon of turmeric
1 Tablespoon of vegan butter
1 Tablespoon of olive oil
Salt and freshly milled black pepper

METHOD

First breakdown your tofu into "scramble" looking pieces. Now heat up your butter and oil together and add your tofu pieces. Cook until the water from your tofu is almost gone.
Now add all your other ingredients and cook for around 5 minutes and then serve'd
Notes
This works really well on toast topped with slice avocado and lashing of black pepper, or, allow to cool and mix with vegan mayo for egg mayo sandwiches!

APPLE CRUMBLE

DELICIOUS HOT OR COLD BUT ALWAYS WITH LASHINGS OF DELICIOUS, CREAMY CUSTARD!

INGREDIENTS

For The Filling

4 Large cooking apples, peeled, cored and sliced.

2 Tablespoons of sugar

1 Teaspoon of mixed spice

(Feel free to add a few raspberries, blackberries or anything else you love!)

For The Topping

180 gms (1 ½ cups) of plain flour

110 gms (½ cup) of sugar

1 Teaspoon of cinnamon

1 Pinch of salt

110 gms (½ cup) of cold vegan butter

Large oven proof dish

METHOD

Heat your oven to 190 (380 Gas Mark 5)

Mix your filling in a bowl, so the sugar and spice is evenly distributed and then lay into your

bowl, tucking down nice and tight.

Now, in another bowl, add your flour and butter and rub through until you have a fine crumb

mix. Now stir in your sugar, cinnamon and salt.

Evenly spread over your fruit and use a fork to create a pattern over the top.

Place into your oven for around 35 minutes, or until the fruit is soft when you put a knife

through, and serve with custard, or ice cream or both!

Note

You can use frozen or tinned fruits too!

THE VEGAN CREAM OF TOMATO SOUP

THIS IS A VERY EASY SOUP TO MAKE AND REALLY DOES TASTE EXACTLY THE SAME AS THAT FAMOUS VERSION

INGREDIENTS

2 Tins of whole tomatoes (get a good quality if you can)
1 Can of water (use one of the tomato tins)
1 Large spanish onion, sliced
4 cloves of garlic, crushed
1 Tin of full fat coconut milk (must be full fat!)
2 Teaspoons of dried italian herbs
Salt and Pepper
2 Teaspoons of sugar
Good slug of olive oil for frying the onions.
Hand blender to create a smooth soup or you can add to a food processor.

2+6= CARRITS

TICk BOx IF u FINK StevE is STOOPID ☑

U can serbe it in a buckit

METHOD

In a good quality, heavy saucepan, gently fry the onions until they are starting to brown (caramelise). Take your time, this adds a great depth of flavour. If they look like they are burning, turn down the heat and add a splash of water to loosen them up, but take your time, it makes all the difference.

Once they are brown add everything apart from the coconut milk and mix through, bring to a simmer for around 2 minutes. Now add the coconut milk and mix through.

Once mixed, blend your soup carefully as it is hot, and then taste and adjust your seasoning. Heat through and serve with crusty, fresh bread for dipping and scraping up the last bits in the bowl!

Notes
You can use fresh tomatoes too, but the tinned variety gives it that authentic flavour, or you can use a mix of both fresh and tinned, both work really well.
For serving: Fresh basil, if desired

MARINATED TOFU SKEWERS

SUPER EASY, JUST TAKES A LITTLE BIT OF PREP WHICH YOU CAN DO THE DAY BEFORE YOU PLAN TO EAT

INGREDIENTS

One pack of firm tofu (must be firm tofu)
Handful of cherry tomatoes
One courgette (zucchini) thickly sliced
Handful of button mushrooms
6 Large Skewers
For The Marinade
Large sealable container (like a lunch box)
120 ml (½ cup) of water
¼ cup of maple syrup

3 tablespoons of soy sauce
1 tablespoon of olive oil
2 crushed cloves of garlic
1 tablespoon of smoked paprika
1 Teaspoon of chilli flakes
1 Tablespoon of ketchup
1 Tablespoon of mustard
A few drops of liquid smoke (optional)

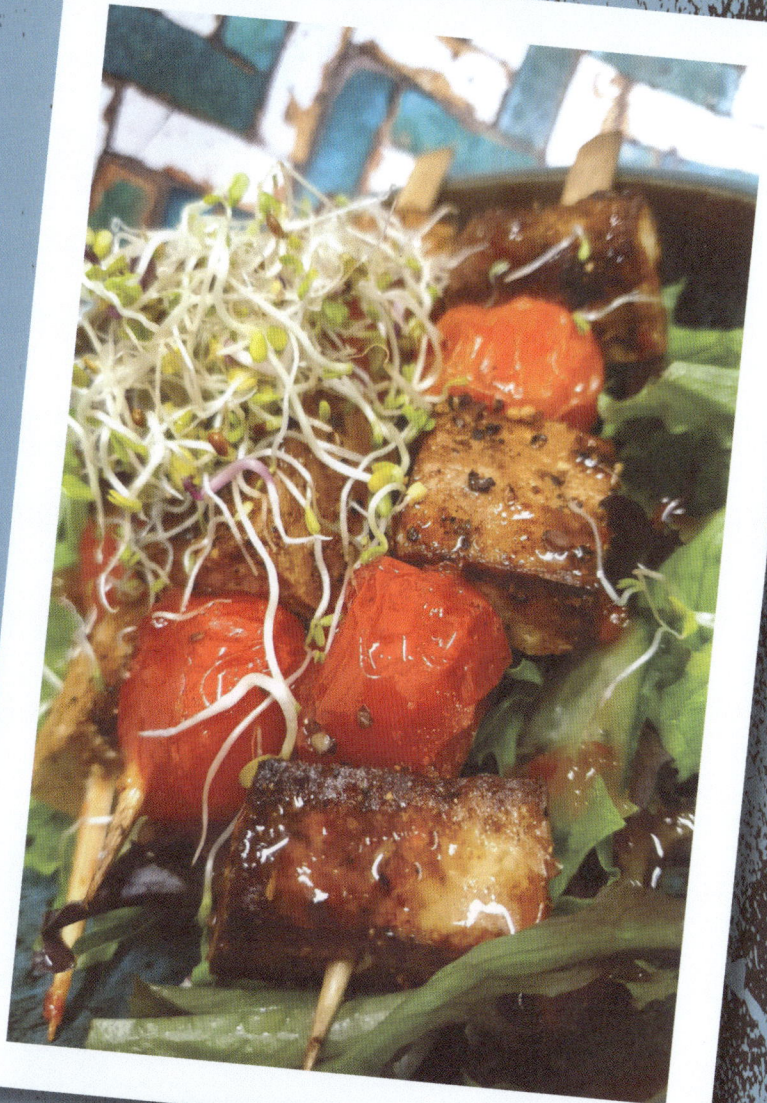

METHOD

First you need to ensure your tofu is pressed, basically removing all the liquid it has been stored in. To do this, just open, drain and then put between several layers of kitchen roll and
load weight on top, such as tins of food etc or, if you have one, put it in a tofu press. Do this
the day before you need the tofu, this way you know you will have a great starting point for
your kebabs.
At the same time, mix together all the marinade ingredients and put in the fridge until your
tofu is ready.
Once your tofu is drained, cube it and place into the marinade. You can leave it in the
marinade for 20 minutes or 24 hours. The longer you leave it, the more intense the flavours.
When you are ready to cook, take your skewers and load up everything onto them,
spreading the vegetables in between.
If you are using bamboo skewers, soak them in water before use to avoid them burning.
You can now cook them, either in a shallow pan with a little oil, or, the best way, in the oven
(200 degrees, 400, Gas Mark 6) or on a BBQ or grill. Use the leftover marinade to baste
them throughout cooking.
Now serve with hummus, flatbreads, or with a salad or in a wrap!

"Ronnie got himself a job at the local restaurant, but the owner, Mr Scrummidindins, ended up crying in the back office because someone kept eating all the orders.."

LASAGNE & BOLOGNESE

USE PRE-MADE LASAGNE SHEETS FOR EASE, BUT YOU CAN MAKE YOUR OWN IF YOU WISH, BUT FOR THIS RECIPE WE ARE USING READY-MADE, BUT EVERYTHING ELSE IS FROM SCRATCH. TAKE YOUR TIME WITH THIS AND IF YOU MAKE IT THE DAY BEFORE IT IS ACTUALLY BETTER, IT GIVES THE LASAGNE TIME TO REALLY SETTLE AND FOR ALL THE FLAVOURS TO MERGE TOGETHER. SO HERE IT IS! THIS MAKES ONE BIG LASAGNE, ENOUGH FOR SIX PEOPLE, BUT ANYTHING LEFT OVER CAN BE PORTIONED AND POPPED INTO THE FREEZER SO FOR THOSE BUSY EVENINGS YOU CAN JUST TAKE A PIECE OUT IN THE MORNING AND IN THE EVENING, WARM THROUGH AND IT'S READY. USE ONE LARGE PACK OF VEGAN LASAGNE SHEETS FOR THIS, BUT ALWAYS BUY TWO PACKS JUST IN CASE YOU NEED AN EXTRA FEW SHEETS FOR THE SIZE OF YOUR DISH!

For the filling you will need:

Glug of olive oil
Two red onions finely chopped
Pack of mushrooms finely chopped
Three cloves of garlic finely chopped
One courgette, (Zucchini) cubed or grated
Four carrots, grated
Two tins of sieved tomatoes
Two glasses of red wine.
Two jars of lentils
Two vegetable stock cubes
One dessert spoon of marmite (yeast spread)
One dessert spoon of dried oregano
One bunch of fresh basil (this is the best option but if you cannot get it a dessert spoon of dried but do try to get fresh)
A cup of nutritional yeast
Water

To make the sauce

Get everything prepped and ready first, makes it so much easier when you cook. Now, in a large pan add a big glug of olive oil, enough to cover the bottom of the pan and add your onions and a teaspoon of salt. Cook until soft then add your garlic, mix and then add the rest of your vegetables. Mix around and then add everything except the nutritional yeast. Top up with water, I use one of the empty tins from the tomato puree. Give it a good mix and then it just simmer quietly while you prepare the sauce. Keep giving it a little stir and after about 30 minutes check the seasoning and add more salt and pepper if required. You are looking for this to reduce down a little, not too liquidy. At the very end mix through the nutritional yeast and set to one side ready to prepare your lasagne. What you now have is the sauce for your lasagne or, you have your bolognese sauce! Two in one.

For the white sauce you will need:

A good glug of olive oil
Two tablespoons of flour
Salt
Freshly milled black pepper
Glass of white wine
Heaped teaspoon of mustard (any will be fine)
Tablespoon of dried oregano
About a litre (a carton) of plant based milk.
Half a cup of nutritional yeast.
Half a cup of ground almonds

I can eat 3 of these at once

To Assemble
In your lasagne dish, add a layer of the lasagne sauce and layer the pasta sheets over and then another layer of lasagne sauce, then more sheets and repeat again so you have three layers of lasagne and three layers of pasta sheets, finishing with the pasta sheets. Now pour over the white sauce covering everything. Give it a little shake and then sprinkle with a little more dried oregano and then pop into a hot oven, 200,(400, gas mark 6) for about 40 minutes or until the pasta is soft, just put a knife through and check it is all soft.
Take out the oven and leave it to stand for about 15 minutes if you are going to eat it straight away so it "sets" a little and makes it easier for serving. Serve with a fresh basil salad and some delicious fresh bread for "mopping!

STEVE IS GReeedi

CARROT HOT DOGS!

YES REALLY! IF YOU TAKE YOUR TIME OVER THE PREPARATION OF YOUR CARROTS, YOU CAN CREATE DELICIOUS HOT DOGS FOR EVERYONE!

I frikkin luv Karits

I MAde this

You will need

6 (or however many you want to make) Carrots, cut them to the length of your hotdog buns!
The Marinade
Boiling water
(enough to cover your carrots)
A vegetable stock cube
  cup of dark soy sauce
  cup of vegan worcester sauce
(or use apple cider vinegar)
2 Tablespoons of maple syrup.
2 or 3 drops of liquid smoke
(optional but makes a huge difference)
1 Teaspoon of yellow mustard
1 Tablespoon of ketchup
1 clove of garlic, crushed
1 Teaspoon of paprika
1 Teaspoon of onion powder

To Make

Cook your carrots until they are just firm, so you can put a fork into them but they are still firm enough to hold their shape. Meanwhile, put all the marinade ingredients into a bowl with a lid, holding back the boiling water. When the carrots are ready, put them into the marinade and then pour over enough boiling water to just cover them. Put on the lid, give it a shake and then, when cool, put it into your fridge overnight. When you are ready, you can BBQ them, grill or griddle them, use the marinade to brush them throughout for extra flavour. Add to your buns with ketchup, mustard, onions in fact, anything you love on your hot dog!
Note: You can freeze the remaining marinade, put it into ice trays and add a cube or two to your vegetables or stews for extra flavour!

STeve STeals ALL My KaRiTs

CARROT AND LENTIL BURGER

THESE CAN BE MADE AND FROZEN AND YOU CAN, OF COURSE, ADD THE PULSES OF YOUR CHOICE, BUT LENTILS DO GIVE A "MEATY" TEXTURE, BUT EXPERIMENT TO FIND YOUR PERFECT BURGER! DO NOT BE PUT OFF BY THE AVOCADO, IT IS THE BEST WAY TO "BIND" THE INGREDIENTS, YOU WILL NOT EVEN NOTICE IT.

I use a bowl as a helmet

You will need (For 4 large burgers)

3 tins of cooked, brown lentils
6 large grated carrots
1 Large onion, sliced
1 Tablespoon of olive oil (A good glug!)
3 Crushed garlic cloves
1 Dessert Spoon of Oregano
2 Teaspoons of paprika
2 Teaspoons of mustard (any is fine)
1 Teaspoon of marmite (yeast extract) optional
Salt and Black Pepper
1 or 2 Tablespoons of plain flour
1 Smashed Avocado

To Make

Fry off your onions in a little olive oil until they are soft, then add in your garlic and carrot. Mix through. Now add your oregano, paprika, mustard and marmite. Mix though and then set aside.
Drain your lentils and put them into a bowl. Add your cooked ingredients and mix through.
Mix through your avocado and 1 tablespoon of flour. If you feel your mixture needs more, add another tablespoon of flour until you have a mixture you can "mould" into burgers. Be sure to season well with salt and pepper throughout.
Once you have the four burgers you can either fry them or, and this always works better, bake them. Pop onto a lined baking tray, drizzle with a little veg oil and into a hot oven. Turn halfway through and then serve in buns with all the usual delicious trimmings!

Note
You can use the same mixture to make "meatballs" just divide them up into small portions and roll them into balls and bake in the same way! Add extras too, such as chilli for a more Mexican style burger!

"Mrs Weston from 39 Grumble Street had to call the police because someone had landed a helicopter in her garden and dug up all her carrots."

CHERRY PIE!

OF COURSE, YOU CAN PICK YOUR FRUIT OF CHOICE, BUT THIS IS SUPER EASY AND CAN BE WHIPPED UP VERY QUICKLY WITHOUT TOO MUCH FUSS!

You Will Need

2 Pack of ready made puff pastry (most are vegan but always check the labels!)
450gms (2 cups) of pitted cherries
130 gms (⅔ cup) of granulated sugar
1 Tablespoon of cornflour
2 Tablespoon of ground almonds
Water and sugar to brush on before baking!
Pie Tin (We used a 9 inch tin)

To Make

Now, the most important part of any fruit pie is to avoid the dreaded soggy bottom, so take time with the first part of this recipe to avoid this!

In a heavy duty saucepan add your fruit and sugar and mix through until dissolved. Now add your vanilla and your ground almonds, mix through. Finally stir through your cornflour and keep stirring until it thickens, remove from the heat and set aside to cool down.

Next heat your oven to 200 (400 or Gas 6) Roll out one of your packs of pastry and place in your pie tin, have enough to fold outside of the tin (this will help with the sealing and avoid sinkage!)
Now roll out the second pack enough to give you a topping. Once your filling has cooled down, pour into the pastry casel Brush the edges of the pastry and place on the topping. Trim of excess pastry.
Use the excess pastry to make decorations for the top of your pie. Once you are happy, place a small hole in the centre (allows the steam out) then brush with water and sprinkle with sugar.
Pop into a hot oven for around 35 minutes, or until your pastry is risen and golden!
Allow to cool a little before serving and this is just incredible with ice cream!

Notes

You can use any fruit you wish, but the important part is monitoring the liquid aspect of your contents, too wet and you have a horrible soggy base, so adjust the cornflour to match your choice of fruit.

CHOCOLATE & HAZELNUT TARTS

You Will Need

Makes 4 Individual Tarts
1 Pack of digestive biscuits
(or something similar)
125gms (½ cup) of vegan butter
(you may need a little more, depending on your biscuits!)
200 gms (1 cup) of dark, vegan chocolate
Teaspoon of vanilla extract
100 gms (½ cup) of icing sugar
100 gms (½ cup) of Hazelnuts
(chopped but hold a few back for decoration)
4 Loose bottom tart tins
(or anything lined with baking paper can work)

MAKE IT NOW AND EAT IT

To Make

No cooking as such involved here, so nice and simple!
First, crush your biscuits to a fine crumb and then melt your butter and stir through until all coated. You may need to add a little more depending on your biscuits but basically, it all needs to be coated with the butter but keeping its "crumb" appearance.
Divide the mixture between your tins, pushing up the sides to create a little dish. If you have any leftovers you can freeze this for another time.
Pop these into the fridge to set. Now onto the filling

In a bowl, break up your chocolate and place in the bowl. Now cover the chocolate with just enough boiling water to cover it. Leave it for a moment and then with a whisk, beat though until smooth. Once it is smooth you can add the icing sugar and the vanilla extract, mix though again.
Now stir through your chopped nuts. Once evenly distributed you can put into your little moulds, top with your whole nuts and pop into the fridge to set!
When ready, release from your tins and serve, these go really well with fresh raspberries!
It's that easy!

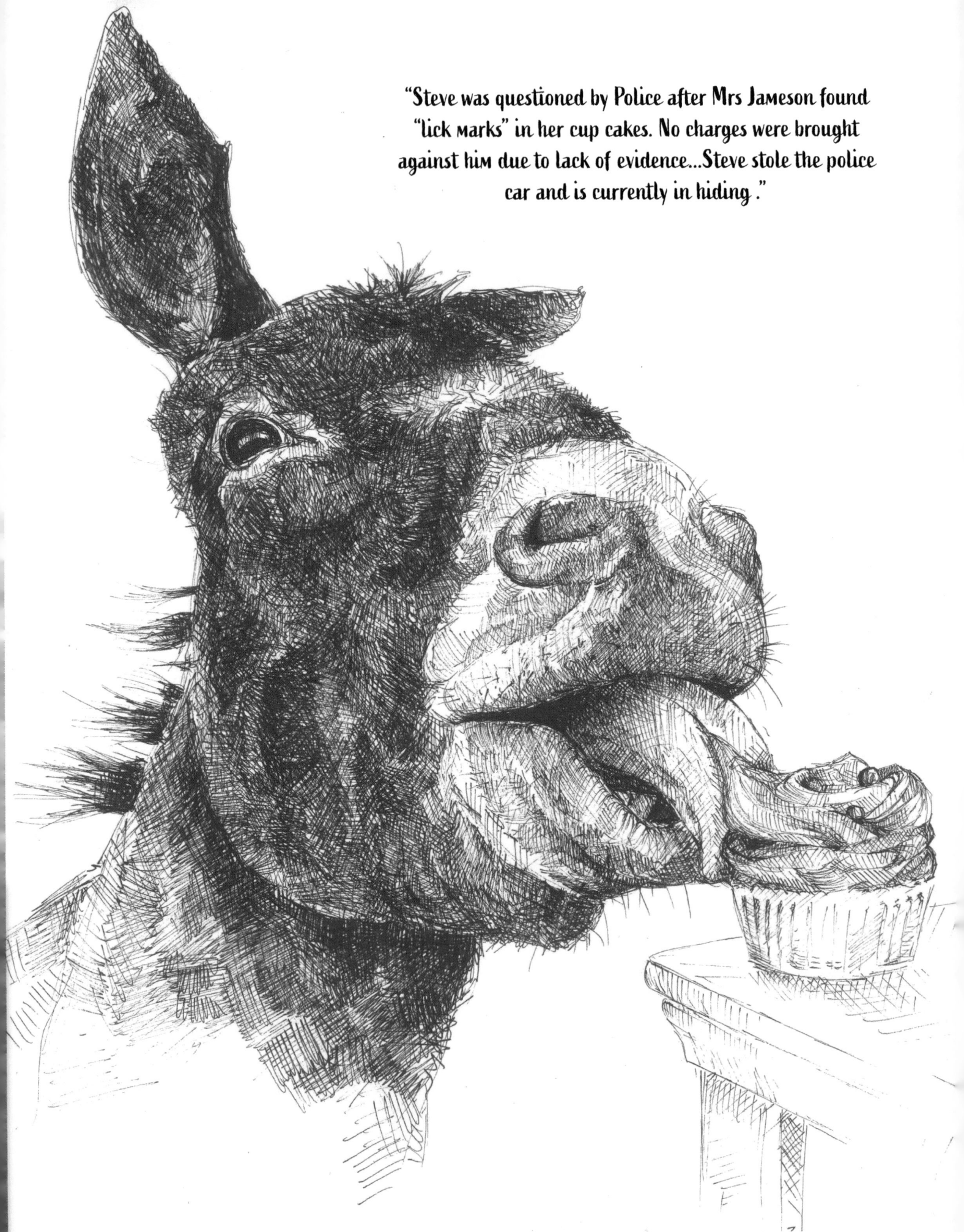

"Steve was questioned by Police after Mrs Jameson found "lick marks" in her cup cakes. No charges were brought against him due to lack of evidence...Steve stole the police car and is currently in hiding ."

Fairy Cakes

You will need

375 gms (3 cups) of Self Raising Flour
200 gms (1 cup) of Caster Sugar
1 Teaspoon of baking powder
1 Tablespoon of lemon juice
100 ml of vegetable oil
170 mls of cold water
Bun Tray
12 Fairy Cake Cases

Decoration

We used butter icing and food colouring, the recipe for this can be found with the Victoria Sponge recipe!

To Make

Heat oven to 180. Place your cake cases in the bun tray. In a large mixing bowl add all the dry ingredients and mix through. Now add the lemon juice, oil and water and mix until smooth. Divide the mixture between the cases and pop into the oven for 12 minutes, then check them by sticking in a skewer. If it comes out clean, they are cooked, if not, leave a little longer and keep checking. Every oven is different so it is hard to give exact times.

When they are cooked through, take them out and leave to cool before decorating.

LENTIL AND MUSHROOM ROAST
THIS IS VERY EASY TO MAKE, FILLING AND DELICIOUS

You Will Need
(Will easily feed 6 people)

4 tins of brown lentils
(or jars)
2 cups of chopped
mushrooms
(any are fine)
1 Leek, finely sliced
1 Onion, finely sliced
2 cloves of garlic,
crushed
3 cups of spinach
3 carrots, grated
1 stick of celery,
finely chopped
1 teaspoon of marmite
(yeast extract)
1 teaspoon of mustard
1 teaspoon of mixed
italian herbs
Salt and Black Pepper
Tablespoon of regular
flour.
A little olive oil for
frying
Baking Tin & Baking
Paper

Notes

This works brilliantly made the day before and heated up before serving. You can also freeze this too, so you an slice into pieces, freeze and take out as needed!

To Make

Heat your oven to 180 (350 gas mark 4)
In a large pan place the oil, your leeks, onions and celery and cook gently until soft. Now add the garlic, mushrooms, carrots, marmite, mustard and herbs and cook gently for around 3 minutes. (you are looking for the moisture to leave the mushrooms)
Now add your lentils, spinach and flour. Mix though and set aside.
Now line your tin with the baking paper and drizzle a little oil in the bottom. Fill with your mix and push down to ensure it is evenly spread.
Now place in the oven for 40 to 50 minutes. Check halfway though and if needed cover the top with more baking paper, but you are looking for something that is almost set. As it cools a little it will set firmer making it easier to cut.
Enjoy with a thick, onion gravy and mash!

VEGAN "FISH" CAKES

FOOD IS ALL ABOUT TASTE AND TEXTURE, SO THERE IS NO REASON TO MISS OUT ON ANYTHING, YOU JUST HAVE TO REPLACE THE ANIMAL PRODUCT WITH SOMETHING ELSE. THESE ARE SUPER EASY, SO TRY THEM. MAKES AROUND 4 LARGE "FISH" CAKES.

You Will Need

To Make The "Fish"
One tin of JackFruit (in brine not syrup)
Two Sheets Of Nori (seaweed)
Juice Of One Lemon
1 Tin of Chickpeas, squashed with a potato masher (save the brine)
Mashed Potato From Four baked potatoes
(bake them in their skins and then scoop out the potato and put into a bowl)
1 Bunch of finely chopped spring onions (scallions)
A bowl of plain flour
(to coat the fishcakes)
A bowl of panko (or bread) crumbs

Note

If you want something a little different, follow the process but create fish balls instead, perfect for an appetiser or snack board!

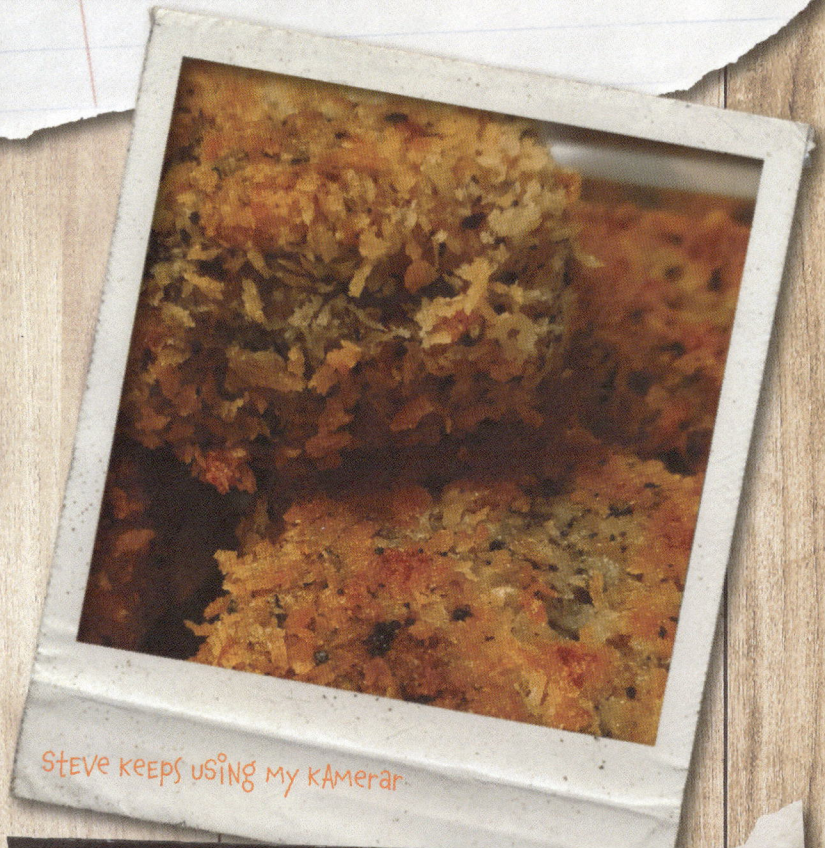

STEVE KEEPS USING MY KAMERAR.

WHAT EVEN IS A VEGAN FISH?

To Make

Heat your oven to 200 (400 , Gas Mark 6)
Line a baking tray with paper and then drain the jackfruit and place on it. Drizzle with a little olive oil and put into the oven for around 15 minutes, just until it is easy to break up the jackfruit with a fork into flakes.
Whilst the jackfruit is still hot, put it into a bowl with the nori sheets (break them up into small pieces) lemon juice, mashed chickpeas and mix through. Set aside for 15 minutes.
Now take your mash potato and add the spring onions (scallions) and mix. After 15 minutes add the shredded jackfruit and chickpea mix into the mash and fold through. (leave the nori pieces in the mix)
Now divide the mixture into four and shape. Place these into the fridge until completely cold.
When you are ready, take each fishcake, dip into the bowl of flour, then the saved chickpea brine and then into your breadcrumbs. Place onto a baking tray lined with paper.
Give them a quick drizzle with olive oil and then into a hot oven 200 (400, gas mark 6) and after 10 minutes, or until golden, turn them over until golden all over.
Serve with a wedge of lemon and a side of vegan tartar sauce and salad!

VICTORIA SPONGE CAKE

You will need

275 gm / 2 ¼ cups Self Raising Flour
200 gms / 3 ¼ cups Caster Sugar
2 Tsps of Baking Powder
Tablespoon of lemon juice
100 mls of vegetable oil
170 mls of cold water.
1 Dessert Spoon of vanilla extract
(not essence)

Filling

135 gms / ⅔ cup of vegan, unsalted, butter
(room temperature)
250 gms / 1 heaped cup of icing sugar
Teaspoon of vanilla extract
Tablespoon of plant milk (to loosen)
Strawberry Jam
2 baking tins, lined with baking paper

To Make

Preheat your oven to 180 (360 gas mark 4)
Line your baking tins and set aside.

In a large bowl add all the dry ingredients
then add the oil and water and mix until
smooth.

Now divide between the two tins and pop
into the oven for 15 minutes. Check with
a skewer, if clean remove, if not give them
another 5 minutes and check again.

Once cooked, set aside to cool before
removing from the tins.

To Make Filling

Put the butter into a bowl and mix, now
add the vanilla extract and the icing sugar
and mix until smooth. If it is too thick, add
the milk, a little at a time, until you get a
"dropping consistency" (in other words
when you get a spoonful of the mix it should
"drop off" the spoon!)

Once the sponges are cool, remove from the
tins, remove the paper and then spread one
side with jam and the other with the cream
and put together. You can decorate the top
with icing sugar but it is ready to eat!

CAKES IS MY BEST FRIEND

Notes

If you want to mess around with the
recipe you can always add mint extract to
the mix and make a chocolate cream filling
by changing 50 grams of the icing sugar for
cocoa powder, or create a chocolate orange
taste by using orange zest in the cake mix,
just experiment!

I LOOK REALLLY GOOD IN THIS PICTURE

"Last Thursday afternoon, Ronnie and Steve went to the shops and found a hat store. On trying out a cowboy hat, Ronnie fell in love with his new look and spent the entire afternoon walking around the shops and looking at his reflection in the windows. In his excitement, he forgot to pay for the hat and was later chased around the streets by a very angry Mrs Farrow who owned the shop. Unfortunately, Mrs Farrow was a little overweight and her trousers didn't fit her very well. Her trousers fell down during the chase and she tripped in front of an oncoming school bus, which swerved into the local cake shop. It was a chaotic afternoon."

CHOCOLATE MUFFINS

SUPER EASY, ONE BOWL, NO OVER MIXING AND THEN EAT WARM OR DECORATE AS YOU WISH

You will need

(use cup measurements for this, so much easier than trying to weigh it all out!)

1 ¼ cup of plant based milk (we use Almond)
1 Teaspoon of white wine vinegar or apple cider vinegar
1 ½ cups of self raising flour
½ cup of cocoa powder
1 cup of sugar (we use light brown but granulated is fine)
2 Teaspoons of baking powder
1 pinch of salt
⅓ cup of vegetable oil
1 Teaspoon of vanilla extract (not essence!)
1 ½ cups of vegan chocolate chips (or you can chop up a bar into small pieces so it can be evenly spread in the mixture)
12 hole muffin tins, 12 muffin cases
Optional
Additional Chocolate To Decorate

I CAN FIT 4 IN EACH EAR

Note

These can be frozen so it can be a good idea to bake a few batches and then just take out what you need and warm through.

Decorating them can be in any way you wish, melt chocolate to create shards, mix up a butter cream with vegan butter, icing sugar and cocoa powder, in fact, decorate anyway you want, but only decorate if you are not going to freeze them!

To Make

Preheat your oven to 200 (400 or gas mark 6) and line your muffin tray with the paper cases.

In a jug add your milk and vinegar and set aside to curdle. Now in a bowl, add all your dry ingredients, leaving out the chocolate chips. Carefully mix.

Now add your oil, vanilla extract and the milk mix and carefully stir. Do not over mix, if you do you will end up with dry muffins!

Now fold through your chocolate chips and then share out among the paper cases.

Pop into the oven and check them after 25 minutes, if you stick in a skewer and it comes out clean they are cooked. Set aside for 5 minutes to cool before decorating or just eat them!

STEVE LUVS POLLY

LENTIL RAGU

SUPER EASY AND WORTH MAKING DOUBLE AND FREEZING

DONKEYS R VERY INTELIJINT

You will need

2 Tins (or jars) of cooked brown lentils
1 Large, finely chopped, red onion
4 Large carrots, grated.
2 Tins of chopped tomatoes
4 Cloves of garlic, crushed
1 Tablespoon of mixed dried herbs
2 Teaspoons of smoked paprika
1 Tablespoon of tomato puree
2 Teaspoons of sugar
Salt and freshly milled black pepper.
Pasta ribbons to serve (or pasta of your choice!)

To Make
In a large, solid, pan, fry your onion, carrots and garlic. Once soft add everything else along with two cans of water (use the tomato cans) and simmer, gently for around 30 minutes.
(This actually tastes much better if you make it the day before!)
Meanwhile, cook your chosen pasta and when ready, drain and mix with a little extra virgin olive oil and then mix into your ragu mix.
Serve with fresh basil leaves, sliced black olives (optional) and vegan parmesan.

Notes
Easy homemade vegan parmesan
Equal amounts of ground almonds, nutritional yeast, garlic powder and a salt to taste.
Keeps in a jar for ages

"I was working in the kitchen making a big pot of tomato soup. Suddenly I heard a huge crash and Ronnie and Steve came smashing through the back door. It seems that they couldn't decide who was best at using the ladel. Ronnie grabbed it and ran off into the garden with Steve in hot pursuit. They both eventually decided that the ladel was rubbish anyway and ate the soup straight from the bowl."

BANANA FLUFFY PANCAKES

THESE WORK WELL AT ANYTIME OF THE DAY, ADD FRESH FRUIT, DRIZZLE WITH MAPLE SYRUP OR CHOCOLATE SAUCE, TRY THEM WITH ICE CREAM TOO

You will need

1 large ripe banana (it must be very ripe)

2 tbsp golden caster sugar
half tsp fine salt

2 tbsp vegetable oil , plus extra for cooking
120g (1 cup) self-raising flour

Half tsp baking powder
150ml oat, almond milk or soya milk

Maple syrup , sliced banana and berries, to serve (optional)

Note
Try with vegan bacon and maple syrup, lemon zest and blueberries, more chopped banana and peanut butter in fact, go wild

To Make

In a large bowl, mash up your banana with a fork, then stir in the sugar, salt and oil. Now add the flour and baking powder and mix through. Now add the milk and mix until you have a thick consistency. It should be able to "plop" off your spoon. Set aside.
Now heat a little oil in a frying pan, you can use plant based butter if you prefer, now add 2 tablespoons to the pan depending on your pan size you should be able to make four at a time. When golden underneath turn over and repeat, they should take about 3 minutes each side.
If your pan is too hot they will burn, so get ready to turn down the heat if you need too. You can pop them into a warm oven whilst you cook the rest of the batter.
Now you can either serve them individually or stack them up with the additions of your choice.

VEGAN YORKSHIRE PUDDINGS

HAVING GONE THROUGH SO MANY EXPERIMENTS TO PERFECT THESE, WITHOUT A TON OF FAFF!, HERE IS THE EASIEST RECIPE

You will need to make 6 Yorkshire Puds

1 cup of plain flour.
1 cup of cold water.
1 cup of plant based milk.
2 heaped teaspoons of egg replacer.
1 heaped teaspoon of baking powder.
Good pinch of salt
1 teaspoon of oregano.
Vegetable oil for muffin tray

To Make

Turn on the oven to as hot as you can so around 220+ Now add a tablespoon of vegetable oil into the bottom of each muffin tray and set aside whilst the oven heats up.
Next put all your ingredients into a bowl and mix well and set aside. Make sure everything is mixed thoroughly.
Now put the tray into the oven so the oil can heat until boiling hot.
Remove, carefully, from the oven after 10 mins and add the mixture evenly. If there is no sizzle on the first drop, put the tray back in the oven to get hotter. This is so important, the oil must sizzle as the mixture hits. Do not take too long doing this, fill, and put back into the oven.
They will rise and when golden, remove from the oven. Every oven is different but around 20 to 25 minutes is normal. You can make these in advance, then place on a tray and just heat through before serving! (you can also freeze these!) Super easy, the secret, a good muffin tray and the egg replacer (available on Amazon)

"Over the past few years, Steve and Ronnie have had some great business ideas and some not-so-great ones. Just last Wednesday I found them planning their next business venture which was for mobile swimming pools and lightweight hammers."

STUFFED SQUASH (PUMPKIN)

THE STUNNING VEGETABLE THAT CAN BECOME A BEAUTIFUL CENTREPIECE FOR ANY DINNER TABLE.

You will need

1 Large Squash
Cup of chopped nuts
Cup of chopped fresh herbs
Juice and rind of one orange
5 grated carrots
Teaspoon of sumac
(optional but it gives a great depth of flavour)
¼ cup of pine nuts
1 Finely chopped onion
2 Cloves of garlic
Olive Oil
Salt & Pepper

To Make

Start by carefully cutting your squash in half long ways and scoop out the seeds and coarse fibres. Set the seeds aside and you can roast these later to use in another dish. Put it to oneside.
Next, in a large bowl, mix together all the ingredients, apart from the oil, and once fully mixed, spoon into each side of the hollowed out squash. Now carefully bring the two halves together and using the string, tie it back together again. Place in an oven dish and drizzle with olive oil, cover with foil and put into a hot oven 200 degrees (400 c or gas mark 6.)
After 30 minutes stick a knife in to see how it is doing, how long it will take depends completely on the size of your squash, but once you feel it soften, remove the foil, drizzle again with a little oil and back in the oven to finish off. Once cooked through, you can slice it into portions to serve with all your favourite veg.

"Like all good crime movies, there is usually a "mastermind". In every single one of Steve and Ronnies escapades there is a shady figure in the background. It is our suspicion that the mastermind behind it all is Dotty, although nothing can be proved. Dotty spends spends her days roaming the spanish countryside flanked by her bodyguards (Barry, Steve and Ronnie)."

By purchasing this book you are supporting Jacobs Ridge Animal Sanctuary. Located in Murcia, Spain, the sanctuary was established in 2012 and is currently home to over 160 animals, including Steve and Ronnie the donkey.

You can further support the work of the sanctuary via the following links

www.patreon.com/jacobsridge

www.paypal.me/jacobsridge

www.jacobsridge.com/shop

follow us on Youtube, Instgram, tiktok and Facebook

Thank you for your support and for purchasing this book. We hope you enjoy it and look out for the next book detailing the escapades of Steve, Ronnie and THE DONKEYS OF CHAOS!

Printed in Great Britain
by Amazon